man with a mission: PELE

Author

Larry Adler

Photography

Bruce Curtis
Joe DiMaggio

 RAINTREE EDITIONS

Printed in the United States of America

1 2 3 4 5 6 7 8 9 0   80 79 78 77 76

Library of Congress Number: 76-11007

Published by   **Raintree Editions**
A Division of Raintree Publishers Limited
Milwaukee, Wisconsin 53203

Distributed by   Childrens Press
1224 West Van Buren Street
Chicago, Illinois 60607

Library of Congress Cataloging in Publication Data

Adler, Larry, 1939-
  Pele.

  SUMMARY: Biography of Pele, the soccer player
who has become an international celebrity.
   1. Nascimento, Edson Arantes do, 1940-
—Juvenile literature. 2. Soccer—Juvenile literature.
[1. Nascimento, Edson Arantes do, 1940-
2. Soccer—Biography] I. Curtis, Bruce,
II. DiMaggio, Joe. III. Title.
GV942.7.N3A65   796.33'4'0924 [B] [92]   76-11007
ISBN 0-8172-0143-2
ISBN 0-8172-0142-4 lib. bdg.

Contents

1

Goodbye Brazil, Hello America

A missionary is a devoted person who travels to a foreign land seeking converts for something he believes in. His task usually is difficult.

He must develop a love and understanding with strangers. He must create excitement for a new idea. He must convince people that the time has come to try something new and different.

Over the years, many missionaries have come to America. But none of them has ever had quite the same job to do as Pele, the Brazilian superstar, the best soccer player in history, the highest-paid team athlete in the world.

When Pele arrived in this country in 1975, he faced a very tough challenge. He was just one man coming from South America. He spoke very little English. Yet he was expected to make soccer a popular sport all across the USA. All by himself.

Soccer wasn't getting a lot of newspaper space in America. It wasn't attracting much interest. Worst of all, it wasn't gaining many fans.

Could Pele change that? Could he make America realize what a great sport it was missing?

He could indeed. Pele's missionary work turned out to be a great success. His presence had an electrifying effect on soccer. People took instant notice of Pele and his game. The proof can be seen where it counts the most—at the box office.

The day Pele signed his contract with the New York Cosmos, more than double the average turnout was on hand for his team's game in Philadelphia. The fans knew that Pele wasn't going to suit up and play. They just wanted to be there to see him wave "hello."

Pele's first game in the North American Soccer League was an international event of the first order. Journalists from 22 countries came for the debut. Twelve nations televised it. Millions of Americans watched it on their TV screens.

The game was played on June 15, 1975, in what was then the Cosmos' home ground, Downing Stadium on Randall's Island, an out-of-the-way spot in New York's East River.

From the first minute of play, excitement and expectation filled the air. Everyone was rooting for Pele to score.

Pele didn't disappoint them. Sixty-six minutes into the game against Dallas, he got his chance. A pass came flying his way. He leaped highest of five men bunched around the goal. In midair, he lashed out with his head like a striking cobra. Thunk! His skull hit the ball and drove it deep into the net. Goal! It was a come-from-behind beauty that tied up the game at 2-2, the final score. The fans went crazy.

Even though the match drew three times the normal crowd, there still were a few empty seats in Downing Stadium. But three days later, for the Cosmos' next contest, the place was sold out. All 22,500 tickets were gone. Thousands of disappointed fans were stopped and turned back at the Triborough Bridge, gateway to Randall's Island.

Then the Cosmos hit the road. Their first away game, in Boston, pulled more than 18,000 fans into a 12,500-seat stadium. The extra thousands spilled onto the sidelines and behind the goal.

Police and guards couldn't control the overflow. After a goal by Pele was disallowed, a mob surged onto the field and surrounded the star. In the confusion, Pele was thrown to the ground and piled on by fans, security men, and officials.

A few Cosmos' hearts skipped a beat. That was their star player at the bottom of that pile! Pele himself admitted that he was "shaken and scared." Although he wasn't injured, he was carried off on a stretcher. It seemed the smartest way to get Pele out of there in a hurry.

"I'm going to make sure of his safety if I have to call in the US Marines," bellowed the Cosmos' general manager, Clive Toye. He liked all those cash customers Pele was attracting. But he had discovered that too many customers could be worse than too few.

From then on, crowd control was better, and the size of the crowds remained just as impressive. The Cosmos drew a record turnout for their Rochester, New York, appearance. They went to Washington, D.C., where Pele met President Ford, and pulled in even more fans for their game there.

Then Pele went off with the team to the West Coast, came back to New York, journeyed to Canada, and returned again to New York. Record attendance figures were chalked up in almost every city Pele played.

Even after the regular season ended, it was still go-go-go for the Cosmos. They took their star and went off on a whirlwind tour overseas. Once again, Pele packed them in wherever he went.

It was all new for the Cosmos, but for Pele it was the same old grind—traveling, making appearances, living out of a suitcase.

It seemed strange that Pele would choose that existence again. The constant traveling and the demands soccer made on his time had been the very reasons he had decided to retire from the game in Brazil.

There, in his native land, Pele played for 18 years with just one team—Santos of the São Paulo league.

Pele was known everywhere. The whole world wanted to see him play. But there was only one way to get him— request an exhibition match with Santos. The invitations flooded in, with the understanding that Pele would come along with the team, of course.

Santos made the most of its opportunities. The club went globe-trotting as often as possible, even though there was a full schedule of league games to be played in Brazil. Santos flew from country to country and continent to continent, knowing that wherever it appeared, it would always draw a good crowd.

Nothing could prevent people from seeing Pele— absolutely nothing. The Biafran Civil War in Nigeria stopped for two days when Pele arrived for a game. Both sides were so eager to watch him play that they called a complete truce!

For Pele, the soccer merry-go-round was both fun and rewarding. He made fantastic money. His annual salary with Santos ran well into hundreds of thousands of dollars. In addition, he received $10,000 in cash for each exhibition game he played. He got checks for endorsing products. He was paid handsomely for participating in a world-wide soccer program for youngsters, which was run by a soft drink company.

He was a multi-millionaire with a long string of investments. He owned a beautiful home where he lived with his wife and two children.

But a businessman must look after his businesses, and a family man must look after his family. Soccer started taking up too much of Pele's time. He realized that when his own daughter didn't recognize him on television. So he decided to hang up his spikes.

"I want to dedicate my time to my family and my business," he said at one point. "Now I'll be able to take my family to the beach," he remarked on a second occasion. And well before his final appearance, to squelch any possible hint of an eventual return, he affirmed, "When I leave the game, it will be for good."

Why, then, did Pele come back a mere 254 days after his self-proclaimed retirement?

Was it for money? Pele's present contract with the New York Cosmos is estimated at $4.75 million. It calls for him to play for the Cosmos until the end of 1977, and then to do promotional work for Warner Communications, the record and movie studio that owns the team, until 1980.

No, Pele didn't sign for money. He already had plenty. He could have relaxed for the rest of his life.

The real reason Pele returned was to carry out a new role in life—to bring soccer to the United States. Pele, the soccer player, would become Pele, the Brazilian missionary to America.

And disregarding everything else—the discomfort of travel, the time away from family and business, the constant drain on his energy—he decided to tackle his new challenge with the dedication and zeal that only a man of true purpose can have.

A look at the history of soccer shows why the game grew so popular almost everywhere else in the world, but never made it big in the United States.

Modern soccer developed in England in the 19th century. At that time, the British Empire extended all over the world. The Union Jack, England's flag, flew from ships docked at ports in every continent.

Like most travelers, the British took along belongings from home, including soccer balls. British sailors kicked balls around harborsides wherever their ships were at anchor. Upper-class Englishmen stationed abroad taught the sport to their friends in other countries.

Soccer quickly spread to many lands. In 1904, a world governing body for the sport was formed in Zurich, Switzerland. It was named the Federation of International Football Associations—FIFA for short. (Soccer is called "football" everywhere but in America.)

Today, there are more countries in FIFA than in the United Nations. Soccer is the most popular sport in the world, and its fans the most hysterical and violent. Soccer riots happen again and again. The worst one was in Peru in 1964. Three-hundred and eighteen spectators were killed in the panic.

Wire fences separating the field from the grandstand are common in South American countries. The players and referees need all the protection they can get. Maracaña Stadium in Brazil even has a moat, just like the kind that used to surround medieval castles. The moat completely encircles the playing field. It is filled with water before each game to keep out possible "invaders."

And for good measure, Maracaña dressing room doors are made of heavy steel to hold back angry crowds that might try to storm inside.

People in other countries are wildly emotional about the game. But until now, Americans never had the chance to develop the same passionate feelings.

How come? Why didn't soccer catch on in the United States when it was gaining popularity everywhere else?

The answer is that Harvard University students of a hundred years ago didn't like the sport.

In the late 1860s and early 1870s, Rutgers, Yale, Columbia, and Princeton all played each other in an intercollegiate game that was something like modern soccer. The ball was round. Players couldn't pick up the ball and run with it or throw it, although they could punch it with their hands and fists. (You can't use your hands at all in soccer, unless you're the goalie.) The ball had to be put through a goal to score.

Harvard, meanwhile, was playing what it felt was a better version of the game, a version in which the ball could be carried. Harvard had to play against a Canadian college, because it had no schools to compete with in America.

Finally, Harvard challenged Yale to a match with Harvard's rules. Yale discovered that it liked its rival's game. The other schools gave the game a try and found out that they liked it, too. By 1876, all the colleges had switched from a soccer-style game to the forerunner of modern football.

Americans more or less forgot about soccer. College and then professional football became popular. Baseball became the national pastime. And basketball, the first American sport, began picking up fans.

But that was before Pele. Today, interest in soccer is soaring, and so are the number of fans. To accommodate them, the New York Cosmos made an important move. In 1976, they returned to what had been their original home ground—Yankee Stadium, which was recently renovated. The rebuilt stadium has 55,000 seats, more than twice the number at Downing Stadium.

The switch was expensive. The cost of renting Yankee Stadium for one game is equal to the cost of using their former home for the entire season. But the Cosmos' management felt it was worth it. "Maybe we won't make any money, but my job was to find a decent place for Pele to play, and a decent place for the fans to sit and watch the game," said Clive Toye. "Now we're putting Pele and soccer in the right surroundings."

The Cosmos also began televising some of their games over two stations. One station broadcasts in English, the other in Spanish. Several other teams are also televising games over local channels.

The more television coverage soccer gets, the happier everyone connected with the sport will be. Television not only brings the game to more people—it also increases revenues, which can then be used to increase salaries.

Ticket sales are up for many clubs in the NASL. And some teams have gone to Great Britain to get their own "Peles"; their own topnotch players from abroad. For example, the Tampa Bay Rowdies signed Rodney Marsh, the San Antonio Sounders picked up Geoff Hurst, San Antonio Thunder got Bobby Moore, and the Los Angeles Aztecs signed George Best and Ron Davies.

A new attendance record, 58,124, was set on April 9, 1976, when the Cosmos met the Sounders in a preseason exhibition game. It was the first sports event at the new Seattle Kingdome.

In addition to everything else, there's been a healthy growth in the number of elementary schools, high schools, and colleges taking up the game. In fact, soccer is the fastest-growing sport in the National Collegiate Athletic Association.

Soccer has a bright future in America. It will continue to grow in popularity. When Pele's work is done and he returns to Brazil, he will leave behind every missionary's goal—a loyal and faithful following. His "converts" will be found in soccer stadiums all over the country.

In the Beginning

Pele was a Brazilian boy wonder. At 15, he was playing professional soccer for Santos. At 16, he was a nationally recognized star. At 17, he was known and acclaimed throughout the world.

Pele was born on October 23, 1940, in Três Corações (which means "three hearts" in Portuguese), a village 170 miles west of Rio de Janeiro. The eldest of three children, he was christened Edson Arantes do Nascimento. His father's name was João Ramos; his mother's, Celeste.

Pele's father, who was nicknamed "Dondinho," also was a soccer player. But his career was jinxed by a knee injury. "I was convinced he was the greatest soccer player who ever lived," Pele has said of his father. "He just never got a chance to prove it."

Even with his bad knee, Dondinho was signed to play for Bauru, a town to the west. He moved there with his family before Pele was old enough for school.

It was there that Pele began playing soccer, barefoot with a ball made out of an old stuffed sock. He loved the game and practiced every day.

He got his nickname when he was 7 or 8, but can't recall why or how. All he remembers is that, at first, he was

puzzled at being labeled "Pele." Edson was his name. He couldn't understand why he should be called anything else.

Pele was a standout in neighborhood soccer games, but he didn't match that performance in his studies at school. He was a poor student who always skipped classes to play soccer. By mutual agreement with his truant officer, he quit school after the fourth grade.

Even then, he knew what he wanted to be when he grew up.

"Soccer was the only career I ever thought of. I worked as a cobbler's apprentice for a while, but I never really thought I'd stick to it."

When Pele was 11, he was discovered by Vlademar de Brito, coach of the Bauru team and a friend of Pele's father. De Brito watched the small, skinny Pele dart around grown men on the soccer field and make them look like fools. The coach realized that the boy was a diamond in the rough. He put Pele on the Bauru junior team.

De Brito spoke in a deep, authoritative voice that scared Pele a little at first. But Pele was a good and eager student, and his coach went out of his way to work with him.

Led by Pele, the Bauru team won the junior championship three years in a row.

Then, despite the fact that Pele was only 14 years old, de Brito decided that his pupil was ready for professional soccer.

Tryouts had to be arranged. De Brito had played soccer in São Paulo, and after getting Pele's parents' permission, he took his student there to be looked over by several teams and coaches.

What they saw was a beardless, bony kid whose ears stuck out of his head like handles on the sides of a jug.

De Brito took Pele to many São Paulo clubs. None was the least bit impressed.

Pele was downhearted. "I was very naive, but I really thought I could make some team."

After Pele turned 15, he went with the persistent de Brito for a trial with Santos. Following the workout, club officials were skeptical about Pele's abilities but reluctantly agreed to hire him. They placed him on the junior team, not expecting much.

The year was 1956. Pele was a young teenager away from home for the first time. In the beginning, he felt lost. He had to live in a club dormitory with teammates who were all strangers to him. And, believe it or not, he was afraid of the dark! After "lights out," the dorm was pitch black.

But in spite of all that, Pele started out with a bang. In his first game, he scored four goals as the Santos junior squad won easily, 7-1.

Opportunity knocked quickly. The Vasco da Gama team in Rio de Janeiro was shorthanded and needed more players for a tournament. Santos lent them four, including Pele. Vasco da Gama won, and Pele was the standout of the team. His sparkling play attracted plenty of attention.

In recognition of what he'd done, Pele was promoted to the Santos first team. It was just three short months after he'd joined the juniors.

De Brito's place as coach and confidence-builder was taken over by the Santos coach, Luis Alonso Perez, whom everyone called "Lula." (In Brazil, everyone in soccer is known by just one name. It may be a nickname, like Pele, Dondinho, or Lula. Or it may be the person's first name or last.)

Lula continued developing Pele's natural ability. Again, Pele listened and learned. From the start, he made a big contribution to the Santos team. In 1957, his first full year in uniform, he put in 17 goals and led the São Paulo league in scoring. He also was chosen to play for Brazil in international matches, where the best soccer players from one country meet the best from another.

Then, in 1958, it came time to select a team to represent Brazil in the World Cup, which was to be played in Sweden. Pele, all 135 pounds of him at the time, was one of the 22 men picked from Brazil. It was a tremendous honor. And Pele was understandably proud.

The World Cup, like the Olympics, is held once every four years. It started in 1930, but there was a long gap in the competition, from 1938 to 1950, due to World War II and its aftermath.

The World Cup is the ultimate in soccer competition. Starting about two years before each Cup, national teams begin battling each other in knock-out competition to determine which 16 countries will meet in the showdown. The 16 teams are then divided into four groups, and each team plays three games in its group. The eight teams with the best records then meet in the quarter-finals, and the elimination goes on from there.

Brazil's interest in the 1958 World Cup reached unbelievable heights. The nation was obsessed with victory.

At that time, Brazil, the fifth largest country in the world, was going through social and economic changes that were turning it into an emerging power in international affairs.

But the Brazilian people were still unsure of themselves and their position. Strange as it may seem, part of this

lack of confidence was due to Brazil's showing in the two previous World Cups.

In 1950, Brazil had met Uruguay in the final for the championship. The largest crowd ever to pack a stadium for a sports event, 199,854, had expectantly jammed the newly built Maracaña Stadium in Rio de Janeiro.

Brazil lost, 2-1. The country was crushed. Some fanatics were so depressed they actually committed suicide because of the defeat!

In 1954, Brazil again entered the World Cup. They faced Hungary in the quarter-finals in Switzerland. In a game marred by fistfights, Brazil lost again, 4-2.

Brazilians felt that their teams' World Cup performances reflected on themselves as an entire nation. The teams had been losers. Therefore all Brazilians were losers.

A World Cup victory in 1958 would give the Brazilians a tremendous psychological lift. It would boost the country's morale. It would tell the whole world that Brazil had arrived. Brazil needed to win for its national pride and respect.

The stage was set for the Cup.

The team arrived at the games with its masseur, doctor, and dentist. A psychologist also accompanied the squad to make sure that it would not only be physically prepared to win, but mentally ready, too.

A few days before the Cup matches, the team went into what it calls "concentration," a way of getting itself in fine tune for the event. During concentration, players are confined and their movements are restricted. Even the food they eat and hours they sleep are carefully checked.

Brazil began without Pele, who was suffering from a swollen knee, one of the first of his many injuries. But the team was strong, and reached the quarter-finals anyway. By then, Pele was ready to play.

The opponent was Wales. The winner was Brazil. And the only goal in the match was scored by Pele, who did it in sensational fashion. The young Brazilian, who had the ball, was standing with his back to the goal. Suddenly, with his right foot, he lifted the ball gently over his head, ducking and whirling while the ball was in midair. The ball bounced off the body of a very surprised Welsh player, who must have wondered what was going on. Pele then lashed out with a left-footed kick and slammed in a goal. From the start of the play to the score, the ball never touched the ground.

Pele scored three goals to lead his team to victory against France in the semi-finals. Then, in the game for the Cup against Sweden, he added some final touches to his amazing display.

Pele fired a vicious blast that took off like a cannon shot. The ball smashed against the uprights with such brute force that it left the whole cage shaking. But there was no goal. The ball rebounded off the cage and back onto the field. Still, it showed that Pele had dynamite in his feet, and it told the Swedes, "Watch out!"

Then Pele scored the first of two goals. He took a pass, juggled the ball on his thigh, and dropped it onto his instep. He flicked the ball over a Swedish defender, dodged around him, then bashed the ball into the net.

His second goal, a header scored just seconds before the game's end, sent Pele sprawling in the mud on the rain-soaked field. Instead of getting up, he just lay there, pounding the ground in a fit of wild joy. The final score: Brazil, 5; Sweden, 2.

After the game, the King of Sweden went down to the field to make what he thought would be a formal presentation of the Cup. But in their moment of triumph, the Brazilians forgot all about the rules that go with meeting royalty. Members of the squad took the king by the arm, embraced him, and got him to pose with them for photographers.

Then the pressure, strain, and realization of what had finally been accomplished hit the Brazilian goalkeeper. He broke down and started to cry. Every other player on the team followed. A candid photograph was taken of Pele at that time. His face was in his hands as he wept for joy on the shoulders of a teammate.

Some of the people in the stands got so carried away that they started crying, too. But then the tears stopped and the crowd began applauding the winners.

In a final gesture of thanks and goodwill, the Brazilians took the Swedish flag and, holding it over their heads, made a full circuit of the field.

The team received a tremendous reception when it landed in Rio. The whole nation was overjoyed. Church bells rang out. Firecrackers exploded. Flags waved. Samba bands danced through the streets. There was a paper storm of confetti and streamers. A half-day public holiday was declared. The Brazilian Congress suspended its session. Over a million people lined the motorcade route from the airport to the Presidential Palace, where medals were given out.

Three months later, Pele celebrated his 18th birthday. The entire course of his young life was completely set, and there was plenty more excitement to come.

Number One

In 1958, the same year Pele played in his first World Cup, he broke the São Paulo league scoring record. He smashed in an amazing 58 goals, more than three times his total for the previous season. It was a fantastic achievement.

Besides his league goals, Pele scored 29 goals in World Cup and international matches with Brazil, and in exhibitions and tournaments with Santos. That gave him a grand total of 87 for the year.

As good as that was, the best was yet to come. The next year, Pele's total goals zoomed to an astonishing 127, another phenomenal record. Forty-five of those goals were scored in league contests, again making Pele São Paulo's leading scorer.

Even though he played with Santos for 15 more seasons, the soccer king was never able to top that incredible total of 127 goals.

In 1959, Pele was still a teenager. His best years were still ahead of him. Why, then, could he never equal the scoring records he set in 1958 and 1959?

The answer is that Pele became a marked man. Due to his talent and fame, opponents began "gunning" for him. They

started using sneaky tricks like holding or shoving to stop him from putting in goals. They aimed vicious kicks at him, since his only protection against injury was his shin guards.

Sometimes Pele shrugged his shoulders and resigned himself to these tactics. He said of his opponents, "They have to do their jobs."

On the other hand, sometimes Pele got even. He has been labeled "the politest fouler in the world," because he's learned how to get back at roughnecks while staying just inside the rules.

The situation bothered Pele, and with good reason. "I've been kicked from pillar to post, particularly in those up-country league games where the home team decided this is the only way to stop Pele and Santos," he once wrote in a soccer yearbook. "At first I was shocked, then I became angry. Sometimes I hit back, and, because my name was Pele, news of such incidents made every newspaper in Brazil."

In one game against Argentina, Pele was continually swarmed by defenders, which was legal, but also grabbed at, tripped, and stepped on, which was illegal. Finally, he couldn't stand any more and blew his cool. In a fit of anger and frustration, he broke a tormentor's nose with a vicious head butt.

Revenge! The Argentinian team took off after Pele, who ran into the rescuing arms of his teammates and countrymen.

Instantly, photographers and journalists poured onto the field, hot on the trail of a front-page story. They wound up sensationalizing the whole incident; blowing it all out of proportion.

One way or another, Pele was always doing something to

make headlines. In 1961, on his way to his fifth consecutive scoring title, Pele scored one of his most spectacular goals. It was so unique, so extra-special, that it was commemorated with a plaque at Maracaña Stadium, the scene of the event. It was also given the name, *gol de placa*—plaque goal.

Brazilians could hardly believe how Pele scored. He dribbled the ball practically the whole length of the field, more than 100 yards, and outfoxed virtually the whole other team, faking man after man out of position.

The goal showed Pele's great skill at ball control, maneuvering, and faking. He can get rid of an opponent in a lot of different ways. He might start dribbling slowly with what looks like great concentration, then suddenly zoom out of sight with a burst of jet speed. Or he might move the ball downfield in a quick, straight line, then stop the ball dead with his feet and instantly switch direction. Without fail, he'll get rid of "tail-gaters," who can't put on the brakes so fast.

During the 1962 World Cup, Pele was able to show only a few of his tricks. He pulled a muscle in an early game and had to sit out the rest of the tournament. All he could do was cheer from the sidelines as his country won the Cup again, beating Czechoslovakia, 3-1, in the final in Chile.

Despite the fact that Pele was of little service to his country during the '62 World Cup, he was of great help to his team during the season. He led Santos to its third consecutive league crown and its first title as best team in the world.

To win that honor, Santos whipped all the best clubs in South America in a special tournament. The Europeans held a similar competition. The two winners met in a best-of-three game series.

Santo's rival was Benfica, a famous squad from Portugal. The first game was played at Maracaña Stadium. Santos won, 3-2, with Pele responsible for two goals. The second and final match was held at the Estadio da Luz in Lisbon. It was one of the best games Pele ever played. He scored three goals and assisted on two others in a 5-2 victory.

During the 1962 season, Santos got direct proof of what a great drawing card it had. A bad injury put their star out of commission for a long spell. Santos' attendance dropped in half.

Pele's value, both at the box office and on the field, was obvious to several rich European teams who wanted the best money could buy. During 1962, rumors started to fly about the possibility of Pele being sold to a team in Europe. Then an Italian team publicly offered Santos half a million dollars for its star. Santos turned thumbs down on the deal. "If we ever sold Pele, we would be lynched," a team official said.

Despite the "no sale," the Brazilian government was scared by the thought of losing its most famous citizen. What was to stop Santos from selling Pele if the price was right? And who knew how high the next bid would be?

Brazil didn't want Pele to leave. So in order to keep him, the president of the country added a new twist to one of Brazil's laws. The law prohibited the sale and export of national treasures such as relics, paintings, and other works of art. The president issued a decree making Pele a national treasure.

Now there would be no more worries. Pele would stay in Brazil—for the next 13 years, anyway.

By this time, Pele had been with Santos long enough to learn the playing habits of the whole squad. He studied and knew all his teammates' moves.

He developed an uncanny instinct. It told him not only where his men were on the field at any particular instant, but also where they were going.

Using this sixth sense, Pele was able to plot complicated offensive plays quickly in his head. And then carry them out on the field.

Soccer doesn't allow huddles or time-outs for a quick word with the coach on strategy or what to do next. Each player has to make his own decisions about how to coordinate himself with the rest of the team. Again and again, a player must check out where his men are and come up with on-the-spot answers to questions like, "Where do I position myself when I don't have the ball?" "Whom do I pass to when I do?" "Should I shoot or not?"

Pele's ability to think quickly gave him the best and most imaginative answers to those questions. His physical abilities helped him carry them out. Pele's mind and body worked together to make him the great player that he is to this day.

As time passed, Pele and Santos kept racking up more achievements. In 1963, Santos again won the championship for best team in the world, beating Inter of Milan in the final, 1-0. It was a vicious game. In the first half, police had to rush onto the field three times to break up fights between players and to protect the referee.

In 1964, Pele scored eight goals in a game, his most ever. In 1965, he made over 100 total goals—101 to be exact—for the third time in his career. Forty-nine of them came in league play, making Pele, as usual, the number one man in the game.

In 1966, Pele again went with Brazil to the World Cup games, played that year in England. Nothing went right. Pele was injured by dirty play and was momentarily so bitter that he vowed never to play in a Cup again. Brazil didn't even make the quarter-finals.

The nation took its defeat so seriously that it went into a state of mourning. Flags all over the country flew at half staff. The team's coach, fearing for his life, didn't return home for months afterward. Brazilians get violent when they think their team has been done wrong.

Pele made his debut in America that year—1966. He played with Santos against Benfica at Downing Stadium. Santos won, 4-0.

The successes continued. From 1967 to 1969, Santos won three straight São Paulo league championships.

The 1970 World Cup loomed ahead. The elimination contests were well underway when a terrible event stunned the sports world—the Soccer War.

The Soccer War was fought between Honduras and El Salvador, who were playing three games against each other for a spot in the Cup matches. The countries alternated home grounds for the first two games. In both cases, the fans' behavior was wild and savage. The countries became so furious at each other that they had border clashes. The third match was played in neutral territory with 1,700 riot-ready police on hand.

El Salvador won the game. Then, to add insult to injury, it invaded Honduras, using tanks and warplanes. Before the shooting stopped, more than 2,000 people had been killed.

There have been many illogical and purposeless wars fought during the history of mankind. The Soccer War ranks high among them.

It was sheer folly. Neither El Salvador nor Honduras had a chance to win the World Cup. To the surprise of no one, El Salvador was eliminated before the quarter-finals. It had the dubious distinction of being the only team to be shut out in every game it played.

Brazil, of course, was also competing in the 1970 World Cup matches, which were held in Mexico. As usual, it had stiff competition.

In Brazil's first game, a 4-1 victory over Czechoslovakia, Pele booted one of his most memorable shots. He missed, but what a try! It was near half-time. Pele had the ball in the center circle of the field, about 60 yards from the goal. Out of the corner of his eye, Pele noticed that the Czech goalie was out of position. To start dribbling toward the goal would put the man back on the alert. Besides, time was running short. So Pele unleashed a tremendous kick. The ball sailed over the head of the scrambling goalie and missed the goal mouth by inches. It was a display of long-distance accuracy that gave everyone something to talk about during the break in the game.

Brazil's next opponent was England, winner of the previous Cup. Well into the game, Pele was dribbling toward the goal. He could have shot and possibly scored, but he didn't. Instead, he faked a move one way, then slid the ball the other. It went straight into the path of an oncoming teammate, who hammered it in. The final score: Brazil, 1; England, 0.

In the third game before the quarter-finals, Brazil came out a 3-2 winner against Rumania. Pele was responsible for two of the goals.

Brazil took its quarter-final match against Peru and its semi-final match against Uruguay. It then had to face Italy in the final. This set up an interesting situation.

When the World Cup competition began in 1930, it was agreed that if any country won the tournament three times, it would take permanent possession of the World Cup trophy.

Brazil had won the Cup twice, and so had Italy. Whoever won the final would have the Cup forever. A new one

would have to be manufactured for future tournaments.

Italy played a defensive type of game. Often it concentrated more on keeping the other side from scoring than on scoring itself. Its men did not like to take chances and controlled the ball using short, safe passes.

Brazil, on the other hand, was more offense-minded. It liked to attack and take the calculated risk. It played a freer, more open game.

The match started out on a field soggy with rain. Despite the conditions, both sides scored a goal by half-time. Pele did the damage for Brazil with a header.

In the second half, the sun began to shine, and so did Brazil. Pele passed for two goals and headed-in a third to make the final tally Brazil, 4; Italy, 1.

A ghost town is a place that's deathly quiet. During the game, Brazil was a ghost country. Streets everywhere were deserted. Nothing was happening. The attention of the entire country was riveted to the game.

When it ended, Brazil went into an uproar. Crowds went crazy. Everyone celebrated. A two-day national holiday was declared. The doors to the presidential residence were thrown open to the public for the first time since the military takeover of the government six years before.

Pele, who already was the only player in the world to score 1,000 goals, now became the only player ever to have been on three winning World Cup teams.

But with the good came the bad. The many years of soccer travel had taken a toll on Pele's personal life. Pele rarely saw his family, and was unable to watch his investments as closely as he would have liked.

So he decided to retire. First, he announced that he would bow out of international competition with Brazil, but would remain with Santos. Later he would take the second step and leave Santos and soccer altogether.

On July 18, 1971, Pele played his last game for Brazil, against Yugoslavia at Maracãna. During the first half, his teammates repeatedly tried to help him score, but without success. This was still an international soccer match. The other side wasn't giving anything away for the sake of sentiment.

At the break, overcome by emotion, Pele ran off the field crying. He ducked into the referee's exit tunnel, where he tried to compose himself. Although hidden from the 130,000 fans at the game, Pele still heard them cheering and calling his name.

A crowd-pleaser to the end, Pele ran back onto the playing area, stripped off his shirt, and waved his "goodbye" to everyone as he jogged around the field. Tears were still streaming down his cheeks.

"It's all too overwhelming," he said in a choked voice as he sat out the second half of the game.

That match marked Pele's 110th international appearance. He'd scored 95 goals in those games. Both are world records. (Just for the sake of comparison, Brazil's second-highest scorer in international matches has 34 goals.)

Pele's last few years in Brazilian soccer were marred by disputes with his club and the national agency governing sports.

A tough bargainer when it came to signing a contract, Pele threatened to quit Santos in 1972 if his terms for a new two-year pact weren't met. The two sides argued for a long time before reaching an agreement.

Then, at the start of 1974, the Brazil Sports Federation appealed to Pele to play in the upcoming World Cup just

one more time. Pele said "no." The organization took Pele
to court and tried to force him back. Its argument was that
Pele, as a soccer player and sportsman, was under its
jurisdiction and thus legally bound to follow its orders.
The case went to Federal Appeals Court, where it was
rejected. The legal battle left everyone with bad feelings.

Pele thought some people tried to get even with him
afterward by barring him from giving TV interviews and
commentaries during the Cup. A Brazilian law forbidding
non-professional talent from doing broadcast journalism
was used to stop him.

As things worked out, Pele had the last laugh. He went to
the World Cup matches in West Germany anyway. There,
as guest of honor at the opening ceremonies, he rode
down the street in an open carriage pulled by ten horses.

Without Pele, and without a powerful team, Brazil was eliminated. West Germany went on to win.

On October 2, 1974, Pele played his last game with Santos. He closed his 18-year career with a combined grand total of 1,220 goals in 1,253 games. No other player comes close to this record. Perhaps no one ever will.

The Pele Personality

In 1975, before he signed with the Cosmos, Pele was conducting a soccer clinic in Malta. The governor and prime minister of the island dropped by to talk. Pele listened politely.

Then, out of the corner of his eye, Pele noticed a kid fooling around with a soccer ball. The boy's shoelaces were undone.

Pele excused himself from the conversation and dropped down on one knee in front of the child. He tied the laces, then looked up at the boy and smiled. After that, he went back to the politicians.

It was the act of a simple, unpretentious man, and that is just what Pele is.

Pele doesn't like people to fuss over him, especially not his friends. If he's at someone's house and he's hungry, he won't ask his host to make him a sandwich. He'll get up and fix one himself.

Pele would rather wait on other people than be waited upon. He's used to doing that. Even at the height of his fame in Brazil, he still played the role of errand boy for Santos, just as he'd done when he was 15. "If I need a soda, Pele gets it for me," a teammate once revealed.

At parties, Pele usually is quiet. He'll kick off his shoes, sit on the floor, and take in what others are saying. He's basically a listener. It's hard to start him talking. But once he does get going, he can speak about almost anything, since he's been so many places, had so many experiences, and met so many different people.

Pele draws attention to himself only if there's a guitar handy. Then he becomes the life of the party. He's a singer, musician, and songwriter who has penned hundreds of tunes. Several have been recorded and have made Brazil's hit parade.

One of his most famous numbers is *Obrigado, Pele* (*Pele Says "Thank You"*). The song shows how humble Pele feels about his accomplishments. In it, Pele thanks his parents, family, country, and the world for giving him everything he has. It's as if Pele were saying that he, himself, really didn't have much to do with his own success.

As a player, Pele never acts the superstar. He wants to be treated just like the rest of his teammates. He once turned down a dinner invitation from a high government official in Belgium because the rest of the Santos players weren't asked (in the end, they were). He said "no" to an audience with Queen Elizabeth when Brazil was in concentration for the 1966 World Cup in England. He didn't want to be the only one on the squad to break concentration. And when he joined the Cosmos, he rejected the offer of a private suite. He asked for a roomate, like everyone else had.

Pele tries so hard to be just like other players that sometimes the results are amusing. After the 1962 World Cup victory, the Brazilian team was celebrating with champagne. Pele doesn't drink. But he didn't want to look out of place. So he got a glass, held it in his hand, and

took sips from it. Nobody knew it at the time, but Pele was drinking water.

Pele feels that he has an enormous responsibility to the public, his fans. That's why he will not endorse cigarettes or alcoholic beverages. That's also the reason he's so generous with his most valuable possession—himself.

Pele has always made himself available to American newspapermen. When he joined the Cosmos, people wanted to read about him everywhere he appeared. Journalists in various stop-offs always asked the same routine questions about his comeback. Pele heard them so many times that he knew them by heart. Yet he never let on. When facing reporters, he acted as if he'd been asked the questions for the very first time . . . instead of the 10th or 20th.

Pele is forever being asked for autographs, and he can't say "no." When he was a boy, he was thrilled whenever he got a player's autograph, and rejected when a player brushed him off. Pele isn't the type of person to give anyone the cold shoulder. He'll sign autographs no matter where or when—even in the middle of a game.

Once, in Brussels, when there was action on the field, a referee pushed a piece of paper under his nose and asked for his signature. Pele shrugged his shoulders as if to ask, "What can I do?" He dashed to the sidelines, scribbled his name, then hastily rejoined the match.

Pele good-naturedly puts up with strangers who walk up to him on the street. On the other hand, he doesn't go looking for attention. Pele has a Mercedes-Benz with the license plate "1000" in honor of his thousandth goal. (A new car comes each year from a German industrialist who is a big fan of Pele's.) Thankful as he is for the gift, Pele rarely uses it. The car draws too much attention. For the most part, he drives a Volkswagen station wagon.

44

Pele realizes that his life will always be filled with intrusions. It's the price he must pay for being a celebrity. For a while, though, he thought it might be different in America.

"When I was here before, nobody knew me," he said. "The United States was like a refuge for me. I could walk on the streets and shop and nobody knew me.

"But," he adds, "now the situation is changing. People are more familiar with me and it's not so easy anymore."

Before he got married, gossip and rumor linked Pele with many different women. But Pele kept his romantic feelings to himself. He felt that his personal life was nobody else's business. Despite being constantly in the public eye, Pele was able to keep his engagement a secret for six years. During that time, his fiancee, Rosie, was never seen with him in public. She never attended a soccer match involving Pele. When the couple was finally married in 1966, it was a small family affair with only one teammate invited to the ceremony.

Years before the wedding, Pele realized that many women would consider him a good catch. Yet he didn't want anyone to marry him for his money. So he said that, whoever his wife would be, she would have to love him because he was "Edson," because of his personality, and not because he was "Pele," a millionaire soccer player.

Pele has his faults, of course. He's human, just like the rest of us.

One person who knows him well says that Pele is cheap—"It is said that when Pele's fist is closed, nobody can open." However, another friend denies it. He tells of Pele's big shopping sprees and his generosity, which some people take advantage of. Some tenants in Pele's apartment buildings live rent free because he won't take them to court for payment.

Pele has made some bad business mistakes because of poor advice. Despite his wealth, he doesn't like losing money. So now his brother, Zoca, a lawyer, handles Pele's legal work, and his circle of financial advisors consists of a very small, trusted group. Having learned from experience, Pele has turned into a very hard-nosed businessman.

Pele knows that Brazilian customs people look the other way when he returns to his country. So he sneaks in electronic appliances and gizmos, which often carry an import tax of more than double their purchase price.

He is crazy about electronic gadgets. His house is full of them. One of his prized possessions is a contraption in his movie room. He just presses a button and the lights go out, the screen comes down, and the projector emerges from the wall.

Pele is not a man to complain. He takes most things in life in stride. Aside from his justifiable grumbling about being knocked around by opponents, Pele has voiced only one other complaint during his entire career. When he first played on American artificial turf, Pele was fooled by how high the soccer ball bounced. He was also confused, he said, because "the ball does not run the same." It was frustrating. Until he got used to things, some of his passes were not as accurate as they would have been on a grass field.

All in all, Pele seems to be a man who is eternally grateful for his success. He looks on what he has been given as a gift from heaven. As one Brazilian put it, "His ability, he says, only God can explain."

end of ch. 9